Choose Your Story

Choose Your Life

Choose Your Story

Choose Your Life

Dean Erickson

Bionic Publishing
Los Angeles, California

Choose Your Story

Choose Your Life

Published by Bionic Publishing
www.bionicpublishing.com

First Edition, 2010

Table of Contents

Dedication and Thanks

Dedicated to:

Dr. Michael Garrett, Dr. Leigh Tobias, Ph.D.,
Mr. Harvard Knowles, and Mr. Art Dyer,
mentors.

*Thank you to everyone who has touched my
life, especially to those who touched it kindly.*

Author's Note and Disclaimer

All opinions expressed in this book are the opinions of the author only. It is not meant to be a medical or psychology primer or text. In fact, the author doesn't much care what the "experts" have to say—unless they are saying something valuable. **Perform the exercises contained herein at your own risk.** The author is not a therapist, trained or otherwise, although he acknowledges he has spent more than his fair share of time with several of them. He is not affiliated with a religion or methodology, any particular group, or much of anything other than his wife and family. He's a man of some life experience and awareness that he wants to share with anyone who might care.

That disclaimed, if this book serves you, please use it. If it doesn't, please read it again. If it still doesn't serve you, maybe you should have written it.

Good luck. (It never hurts to be lucky.)

Introduction

As a physician and wellness practitioner, I meet many people who suffer physical illnesses resulting from living lives that are not fulfilling. They need to make changes, but lack a plan for making lasting change in their lives.

What struck me as refreshing about *Choose Your Story, Choose Your Life* is its rare honesty, so let me be equally honest: if you want to be coddled and told you can get what you want without doing the work that causes that result, this isn't the book for you.

There are many self-help books on the market today that claim to be a remedy for what ails us; lots of discussions about the pressures of the modern world, and all the "tricks" we must learn in order to better cope with it. And then there is *Choose Your Story, Choose Your Life*—a book that tells you what you *need* to hear, not just what you *want* to hear. No more wishing, no more excuses.

This deceptively brief "life guide" (my phrase, not the author's) goes beyond the simple recognition phase of improving one's life and takes you to the most important step—the one that makes the difference. It shows you how to rethink, rebuild and *live* the story of the life of your choosing.

—Cynthia Ambres, M.D., M.S.

What's Your Story?

Forgiveness is the key to action and freedom.
Hannah Arendt

*Life appears to me too short to be spent in nursing
animosity or registering wrong.*
Charlotte Bronte

*To be wronged is nothing unless you continue to remember
it.*
Confucius

*Holding on to anger is like grasping a hot coal with the
intent of throwing it at someone else; you are the one who
gets burned.*
Buddha

Things past redress are now with me past care.
William Shakespeare

*Wanna fly, you got to give up the shit that weighs you
down.*
Toni Morrison

CHAPTER 1

"I am the sum of my parts and experiences, but some parts and experiences are better than others."

What's Your Story?

You have likely been asked this question before in these or similar words. Your answer undoubtedly varied depending upon the asker, the time and place, and your mood. Asked by a handsome guy at a bar, a young woman might deliver a clever response intended to continue the conversation. If the guy wasn't as appealing or the same woman was worn down by a difficult day at work, she would likely respond in an entirely different manner. Asked the same question at a job interview for your dream job, you would probably respond enthusiastically with a well-considered story about your successful work history, achievements, and ambitions. Asked the question while interviewing for a temp agency job, your story might differ as well as your delivery.

Your story depends on the situation. Thus, your story changes or, more precisely, we have many stories, and we tell them in countless ways. Sometimes we make a conscious decision about which story we tell and the manner of its telling. Sometimes our subconscious dictates what comes forth for complex reasons beyond the scope of the book. But we always have a story milling around in our heads ready for the telling, either to ourselves or others.

Let's begin our exploration by looking at three different stories about a man's life history, each told by a middle-aged man.

Here's a story from Mr. A:

I grew up in a beautiful, small town. It was a great place to grow up; very safe, the type of place where you could go trick-or-treating or ride your bike all over town and not have to worry. I'm the youngest of four children. Because my siblings had already broken my parents in I could do pretty much whatever I wanted, but I was a good kid anyway; a good student and athlete. My brothers used to take me to play football with their friends even though they were five and seven years older than me. I couldn't really compete with the older guys, but I loved being out there with them. We played basketball together, too. I'd challenge them both and actually thought I could beat them, one against two. It was great fun. I remember our dad hitting fly balls to us in the front yard and me playing baseball with my buddies on the bigger lawn near the duck pond. The only problem playing there was that a foul ball might plop into the pond. Then, I'd have to go wading to retrieve it. It was pretty hilarious and a small price to pay for a good ball game with my friends.

I graduated near the top of my high school class. Our team won the state basketball championship my senior year, and I was selected to the All-State first team. Everyone knew me; I was a big fish in a small pond. After high school, I chose to go to a prep school to better prepare for college. I had always been a good student, but now I felt like I was really learning! I still excelled at sports and was named MVP of the basketball team as well as All-League in lacrosse the first year I'd ever played the sport, but the educational experience better prepared me for college and later success.

After prep school, I went to Brown University in order to benefit from a great academic college, but one which was situated in a small city where I wouldn't feel overwhelmed. It was a great choice. I met people who are some of my best friends to this day at Brown; it's an incredible school. You could do so many different things, study whatever you wanted, and be whomever you wanted. There was something there for everyone, and I imagine there still is. I played some lacrosse, but I concentrated on basketball and started for the varsity during my sophomore and junior years. I even made an All-Tournament team in 1980 with future NBA superstar Isaiah Thomas. Not bad for a small-town kid. Because I'd completed my academic requirements in only three years, I took a semester off as a senior and didn't play ball that year. I've been best buddies with my college roommate since freshman year of college and am godfather to his beautiful and talented daughter. I'm very proud of her, just like I am of my wonderful nieces and nephews. Definitely, my college years have been of lasting importance to me.

After graduation, I moved to New York City where I worked for several years, first as an options trader, then as a risk arbitrageur. It was exciting stuff. I worked in high-yield bonds and also for a big broker who ran a hedge fund. Wall Street finance is a fascinating business, and I learned a lot and made good money, but I was ready for a change after six years. I just didn't know how big a change it would be.

I decided to take an acting class in order to become more comfortable in sales and got hooked. What a blast! Acting was 180 degrees from Wall Street, but it was wonderful, in its own, very different way. I was in store for great fun for years to come. I took classes from the likes of Uta Hagen, Anne Jackson, and Victor Garber, and met interesting, motivated classmates, including future stars, Amanda Peet and Hope Davis. I performed in lots of theatre productions around Manhattan. I probably did ten to twelve plays, ranging from Shakespeare to brand new works, in just a few years and felt like I was going to change the world with every performance. I gave it my all and loved every second. I even worked in Hollywood for a few years, guest starring on a television show, along with some other jobs.

Then I did a 90 degree turn, not a whole 180 this time, and became a writer. I woke up from a dream one night and just started writing. My dream was so vivid I felt I had to capture it. Then I kept writing until I had finished my first screenplay. Writing was something I could do anytime, unlike acting, and still be creative, so I loved it. I probably wrote eight screenplays and a few sitcom episodes until I got the big idea of writing a novel. Ha! What was I thinking? The result has probably been one of my greatest accomplishments, not necessarily because it's my greatest work (I'm still partial to what our high school basketball team accomplished), but it takes a lot of perseverance to follow through on such a difficult task. I kept going despite several months-long lulls during the writing process. No one else even knew I was writing a novel, so I wouldn't have been ridiculed for quitting, but I had set out to write the whole story, not just part, and I did. I'm very proud of that accomplishment and think it's a damn good story filled with memorable characters.

Last, but not least, I got married after the age of fifty to a lovely, kind, supportive, and successful woman with whom I look forward to spending the rest of my life.

I've been incredibly fortunate, though I wish I could do it all again. I'd have even more fun!

The following is a story from Mr. B:

I have some good and bad memories from childhood, but feel like I've blocked a lot out. Maybe I've chosen to forget, because there always seemed to be so much tension in the house. I was the youngest by many years and often felt like an afterthought. Because my brothers and sister were out of the house by the time I was a teenager, I spent a lot of time by myself. Sometimes I'd spend hours in our basement dribbling my basketball alone and listening to music. As I recall, we only had six or seven records. Fortunately, most of them were made by the Beatles. They made a big impact in my life.

I was a very good baseball player as a kid, making Little League and Babe Ruth All-star teams, but I hurt my elbow during junior high. I was a catcher, and it hurt so much to throw I could barely get the ball down to second base. Some knowledgeable people thought I could have become good enough to play pro baseball, like one of my not-too-distant relatives had done. When I hurt my elbow, that possibility went out the window. Too bad: it would have been nice to play sports and make a lot of money. Instead, I have to work for a living like most everyone else.

High school was funny, but not always in a good way. I mean, I did well and everything, and mostly had fun, but I remember always feeling scared. I felt like a fraud, like I would be found out for something. What, I didn't know; just something. I was awkward and scared with girls. Of course, it's no wonder: the totality of my sex education derived from a circa 1950s book my mom gave me to read. I had friends, mostly from sports teams, I but didn't have anyone to confide in about my insecurities.

Fortunately, my grandparents on my mom's side lived right down the street. My parents argued a lot, and my mom had kind of checked out emotionally, so I spent a lot of time with them. They were the best. I'd sometimes eat three meals a day there and have snacks of freshly made cookies, too. Their house was my safe haven growing up, and I always felt welcomed. Although they lived good, long lives, I was still devastated when they died. My grandfather passed first, and I had never cried so hard in my life. I felt like my world had ended. I can still picture him in the hospital, hooked up to tubes, unable to speak, crying. I wish I had told him I loved him before he died, but I didn't want to be too emotional at the hospital, so I didn't. Besides, that just wasn't something men in my family said. He had never told me he loved me either, but I knew he did. And I think he knew I felt the same for him. It's still one of my big regrets though, that I didn't tell him. Anyway, I was around thirty when he died, and I was bawling my eyes out at his funeral, unable to stop. Maybe I cried so hard because he represented that safe haven from childhood. *How would I ever feel safe again?* I blubbered the same way when my grandmother died a year and a half later. I still miss them and feel like crying as I write this. I guess life goes on—at least, it does until it doesn't.

After college, I worked in finance, but left after several years and somehow stumbled into becoming an actor. I struggled to find enough work and became a writer, but then I couldn't find any paying work. It probably wasn't a clever career move going from one nearly impossible profession to another, so I became a personal trainer to pay the bills, but then I hurt my back and had to stop. I was only forty at the time and had always been athletic and physically-oriented, so it was difficult adjusting to the pain and my reduced abilities. Now, after ten years, I still struggle with back, hip and leg pain and regret the day I decided to become a trainer. Ironically, training turned out to be a waste of my good health, but I had needed the money. Ultimately, I wrote a mystery novel that few people have read, some of it written while lying on my stomach because I couldn't sit in a chair for more than five minutes at a time. Sometimes, I wish I'd just stayed in finance, but know I would have been either rich or dead by now. My complete misery wasn't worth the potential money. Although I came back into the investment world with my own firm, and enjoy the business now, I still am uncomfortable selling. At least, with my experience, I understand risk and portfolio management well, which is unlike many investment people who are simply stuffed suits paid to sell and can't take care of their clients once they do.

I have some regrets, like I never got rich, but I guess I've done alright with the hand I was dealt.

Mr. C's story is next:

One of my earliest memories is riding a lawn tractor with my best friend and my father. I was eight years old. We rode around our house and, as we were going up a hill in our backyard, my father told me to pull back on the gear shift. At least, that's what I thought he said. Anyway, I pulled back the shift and the tractor flipped over backwards. My dad and I fell to one side and my friend fell to the other. Fortunately, we weren't crushed, but my buddy hurt his hip and was in a wheel chair for a while. Afterwards, I cried my eyes out fearing that I'd badly hurt my friend. I remember crouching in the bathroom, bawling. Everyone knew where I was, but no one came for me. When I finally came out, no one comforted me. No one said much of anything. I felt like it was my fault. I mean, I did move the shifter, which made the tractor flip, so it was my fault. *Right?* My father wasn't one to take responsibility for anything he didn't like.

When I was thirty or so, my mom told me I had been a *pleasant surprise* as a baby. My two brothers and sister were born within four years of each other, and I came along more than five years later. What my mom really meant was that *I had been a mistake*. I had never felt wanted growing up.

Another time, probably trying to assuage her feelings of guilt, she told me she had tried to stay in her bad marriage until I was eighteen and out of the house, but she could only last until I was fifteen. Telling me only increased my own guilt, because I had sensed her unhappiness at the time. Kids know these things, even if they can't express how they feel about them. Frankly, I'm glad she left when she did. I couldn't have withstood three more years of yelling, screaming, and hatred spewing through the house.

Although I don't remember it consciously, I've been told that about one month after my birth I contracted pneumonia. My parents were on a weekend trip, so the four of us kids were with my grandparents. I was taken to the hospital where I was kept in an oxygen tent for three days. They tell me I almost died. To this day, I suffer from bouts of claustrophobia and wonder if that symptom started from my experience of being trapped in an oxygen tent barely able to breathe. I've also wondered more than once whether everyone might have been better off had I died in that tent.

My father was a drinker, and he wasn't usually a pleasant drunk, especially as the years wore on and my parents' relationship deteriorated. He would yell and call people stupid, especially those who worked for him. And I was one of those who worked for him, because I had to. I started working weekends when I was around seven or eight. I hated waking up early on Saturdays and still do. Even though I was never called stupid, I always felt stupid. Nothing I did seemed good enough, so I became my own harshest critic. If something wasn't perfect, it sucked. If I wasn't perfect, I was no good at all. I felt no appreciation for normal things, only the absolute best. And what was best? *Who knows?* Living like that was exhausting because I could never give myself a break or cut myself any slack. It's still hard for me to do. My dad had opinions on everything and everyone and they were inevitably negative. My opinion about myself simply mirrored his general attitude.

I guess I was lucky in one way. He only hit me once, and it was only a shot on the arm, but I always felt afraid of him. I know my mom was scared of him, too. Now, I understand he probably yelled to cover up his own insecurities, but I doubt that knowledge would have helped either mom or me back then.

After college, I worked on Wall Street, because that's where the money was. I remember wanting to get rich and retire to a deserted island by the time I was thirty. In my experience, people could only make you feel bad. I wanted nothing to do with them, other than for sexual relationships and half-hearted attempts at love. I probably worked on Wall Street to impress my father, but I was miserable and didn't last long. I've bounced around in a bunch of jobs and professions since then, mostly avoiding too much responsibility.

I've had my share of health issues, too. When I was eleven, I got some sort of staph infection in my foot and it precipitated blood in my urine. I mean, I was peeing brown. It took about fifteen years to diagnose, but I've had a kidney disease since childhood. Recently, due to being prescribed the wrong medicine, the disease has gotten worse. I take prescription pills daily and have dietary restrictions, but they're nothing compared to my bout with cancer a few years back. My doctor kept treating a lump in my neck as an infection, but I started having panic attacks and trouble breathing. Well, the lump was pressing on my neck, so, of course, I was having trouble breathing. Finally, I got to the right doctor who diagnosed the lump as cancerous; something called acinic cell carcinoma. An operation that removed my salivary gland and subsequent radiation treatments seem to have cured the cancer. Being strapped to a table, motionless, so they could radiate my neck and face thirty-three times was tougher for me than the original operation. At least, I was unconscious for the surgery.

Anyway, I'm almost fifty-two, with a bum back, numbness down my right leg, kidney problems, and a history of cancer. Sometimes I'm glad my life is more than half over.

So, we've heard from Messrs. A, B and C. With which person would you rather spend an afternoon? I suspect (and hope) most people would prefer Mr. A. He's upbeat and seems to have a sense of humor. He would likely be a supportive friend and someone you could trust with a secret. You might enjoy sharing a laugh, or a beer, with him, and he'd probably have something interesting and positive to say. He wouldn't try to bring you down, but would likely encourage you to realize your best self.

We've all experienced someone like Mr. C, someone who always has a tale of woe at the ready. Hopefully, you don't have to experience him for long, because listening to Mr. C grows old quickly. He is happy to drag you down into his own life muck and is the epitome of the phrase "misery loves company." HIs love isn't for you, however. It's just for himself and his unhappy story. If he can get your attention, he becomes validated in his "poor me" self-indulgence. His self-worship thrives on the difficulties he's survived. By listening to him, you help convince him he must be special, but you don't help him get out of his own muck so he has a chance to thrive and live a more hopeful life. Left to his own devices, he'll be forever stuck. His motto is probably, "Look at me. Look at what I've survived. I must be special!" His "specialness" is something he needs to believe, because, deep down, he doesn't believe he's special at all. His subconscious self is telling him a nasty story, and he simply affirms it day after day by re-telling it.

How about Mr. B? He seemed alright. Didn't he? He loved his grandparents, after all, but he didn't seem to have much enthusiasm for the rest of his life. He sounded like a victim—not nearly as bad as Mr. C—but he still didn't appear in control. He seemed to be floating in the breeze, waiting for the end of his journey, rather than actively creating his journey. It's hard to know from his story what he even wanted. He and his life appeared colorless and joyless. Most people avoid someone like Mr. B, once they figure out what he's about.

Now that we've met our subjects, let's look at their stories in more depth.

The Good, the Bland, and the Ugly

You may be disappointed if you fail, but you are doomed if you don't try.
Beverly Sills

An ounce of action is worth a ton of theory.
Friedrich Engels

Even if you're on the right track, you'll get run over if you just sit there.
Will Rogers

The man who has done nothing but wait for his ship to come in has already missed the boat.
Anonymous

I am not bound to win, but I am bound to be true. I am not bound to succeed, but I am bound to live up to what light I have.
Abraham Lincoln

Heaven ne'er helps the men who will not act.
Sophocles

CHAPTER 2

"I was very proud when I realized I can accomplish the difficult until I realized little is easy."

The Good, the Bland, and the Ugly

As you may have guessed, Messrs. A, B and C represent the same middle-aged man. Each story is true and unembellished and is mine. That's right. Mr. A is me. As is Mr. B. Unfortunately, so is Mr. C.

We all have stories, countless ones, that we tell ourselves and other people, some more at the ready than others. Some stories are told consciously and some spew forth from our subconscious. We have stories that support us and others that tear us down or keep us bound wherever we are.

I love my A story. There's a lot of cool stuff in there. Man, what a good life I've had and have!

My B story is okay; it could be better and could be worse. It's great to remember my grandparents, but most of my memories of them belong in my A story. They were wonderful people and their influence remains a big part of who I am and will be. I was fortunate to have them in my life for so long. The other events are fairly nondescript and difficult to remember only days after I wrote my B story. Talk about bland!

What about my C story? It is all true, as I recall, but it's only one story. It doesn't represent my totality, and it doesn't have to guide my life moving forward, especially if I don't reaffirm its power by telling everyone I meet my tale of woe. I don't have to wallow in that story or live the hard luck life it implies. I can choose not to be a victim of that ugly story. Many people have overcome much tougher circumstances than mine and, probably, yours.

Look at Oprah Winfrey. Forgive me for jumping on her already full bandwagon, but what she's accomplished and what she embodies as an empathetic person are amazing. She's been very open about the poverty and sexual abuse she suffered early in her life, but she hasn't let those events and that story define her. She's created a better, more life-affirming story and continues to create it every day. You likely are aware that she's creating her "own" television network. How many people have done that? And she's succeeded by sharing her talents and gifts with others. She's a generous philanthropist, and millions of people have benefited from her life and television show. Had she wallowed in her early C story, I doubt she could have accomplished all she has. She moved beyond her early story to create a better one and became a major, positive influence upon the world. Hers is an amazing A story, and she lives it every day. But she has B and C stories, too. How did she escape their clutches? Why doesn't everyone live in their A story and just leave their B and C stories in the past where they belong?

Consider Stephen Hawking. He is a groundbreaking physicist and author of several books, including *A Brief History of Time*, which made physics accessible to millions of laypersons. He has accomplished all of it while living with ALS (also known as Lou Gehrig's disease) since his early twenties. You may have seen him on television, in his wheelchair using a speech synthesizer in order to talk because his musculature was no longer under his control. I can't even imagine the difficulties of coping with such a condition, yet he's affected the world in immeasurable, positive ways. He didn't wallow in his C story and health issues. He took his A story, his brilliance and desire to help, and offered himself to the world for its benefit.

Bill Clinton is another example of moving far beyond one's early story. He grew up in a rural Arkansas town with an abusive, alcoholic stepfather, after his real father died in a car accident before his birth. Difficult circumstances for anyone, for sure, but he didn't live that unfortunate story; he created a greater story for himself. Unless you've grown up in an alcoholic family, you might not understand how difficult it can be to escape alcoholism's clutches, but he became a Rhodes Scholar, governor of Arkansas, and the 42nd president of the United States. Currently a philanthropist and respected statesman, he has lived an amazing A life after a precarious beginning.

None of my examples are perfect by any means; each of us may be aware of lesser moments in their histories. We all have them, folks. But why focus on those? Does that make you feel better about your own life? How? Why? Judging others or comparing yourself in any way is a waste of energy and can only hold you back from reaching your potential and living your own A life.

I didn't focus on their B and C stories. More importantly, they didn't either. Had they, they would have had no time or energy for much else and no way to live up to their A potential.

Few people will experience success the likes of a Stephen Hawking, Bill Clinton, or Oprah Winfrey, but you can experience *your* success. Focusing on your A story will help you by building your confidence so you *dare* to pursue your dreams and goals. Belief in one's abilities and worth supports the perseverance often required to accomplish difficult tasks. Belief in oneself may allow you to speak onstage, strike up a conversation with an attractive stranger, or create your dream job. Short of just being lucky—hardly something to depend on—only by taking action and trying to succeed will you succeed. Your A story supports you in every positive endeavor. Wallow in your C story by telling it again and again to yourself and others and you will probably live only a C life, because that's what you will come to expect. *Snap out of it!* After all, if you spend your life complaining, you'll probably be surrounded by complainers. *Who else would listen?* If you live your life thinking about the worst things you've experienced, you'll convince yourself that your worst is normal, and you'll likely get more of it. *You deserve better!* Focus on your A story, and you're far more likely to leave your B and C stories behind to live the A life you deserve.

I'll teach you how.

I invite you to do the following exercise, **but if any part of the exercise feels emotionally overwhelming, please stop and seek professional counseling.**

Grab a pen or pencil. You may wish to get a few pieces of lined paper, or you can write your answers in this book—*your book*—in Appendix B. You may also use a computer, just be able to write answers as quickly as they come to mind. When you're ready, answer the following questions, keeping in mind there are no right or wrong answers. Write a word or a few words, but don't go into detailed description. That will come later.

What are the three *best* things or events that have happened in your life?

What are the three *worst* things or events that have happened in your life?

What are three *other* things or events that have happened in your life?

For examples, see Appendix A, but please try to answer the questions first. When you're finished, build on the exercise by adding three more answers to each question.

By now, you have listed six *best*, six *worst*, and six *other* things or events that have affected your life in some way. Please don't judge them. Your answers can't be right or wrong; *they simply are*.

The exercise is about to get more interesting. On separate sheets or on the pages in Appendix C, expand your list of the six *best* into full sentences, paragraphs, and your A story. No need for artistry; just keep it simple and write as quickly as possible. Write whatever comes to mind. Simple sentences will work fine.

When you're done, do the same for the *worst* (C story) and for the *other* (B story) categories.

Once your three stories are complete, continue the exercise when ready by reading them—out loud, if you can. Start by reading your A story. How does it affect you? Does reciting the best events of your life brighten your mood? Or do they make you feel uncomfortable? Read your A story aloud several times, and notice exactly how you feel. Does anything change with each reading? Make mental or physical notes of anything that comes to mind.

After a short break to clear your mind, read your C story. Consisting of the worst events of your life, how does your C story make you feel? Does speaking that story hurt your mood? Or does it make you feel special in some way? Be as specific, open and courageous in your analysis as you can. How do you really feel? Read it several times, and note if you begin to feel differently with each reading. Take notes. Again, there is no right or wrong answer; *there simply is*.

After another short break, perform the same analysis while speaking your B story. How do your *other* events make you feel? Does one event trigger a stronger emotion than others? Is it positive or negative? Read your B story aloud several times, and see if any feelings change and note how they do. Do you feel like any of these events belong in either your A or C stories? Do events from any story belong in another one? Simply move them and cross out what no longer belongs, so your stories make the most emotional sense to you.

Congratulations. By working through your A, B and C stories, you've done a lot of self-analysis and may have made several discoveries. I know certain life events and my feelings about them were illuminated for me when I did the exercise. I trust the same happened for you. Did certain events hold more emotional impact than you'd expected? Did other events, perhaps silently fretted about for years, have no power whatsoever? After performing the exercise, do you feel that you know yourself better? Hopefully, you answered yes, but you aren't done yet. We do live a whole lifetime, after all, so there can be a lot to learn.

Be kind to yourself and take a well-deserved break to digest what you've experienced, then come back to this point in the book when you're ready to continue.

> ***God helps them that help themselves.***
> Benjamin Franklin

You may benefit by going deeper into the exercise and adding to your lists. Try listing a total of the ten *best*, ten *worst*, and ten *other* things or events, and then expand each into cohesive stories. Remember, they don't have to win an award; just do the best you can. Once completed, take a break, and then read each aloud as you did before. Start with your A story, then read C, and finish with B. How do they affect you now? Do you feel anything different in reading your stories compared to your first reading? Do they hold the same power or are they just stories? Are they powerful or are they becoming more like reading a book or watching a movie?

Feel free to add more things or events to your first ten in each category. Again, turn your larger lists into sentences, paragraphs and stories while adding further detail. Add the new items into your story wherever they feel right to you. Chronological order is fine, or arrange them however you see fit. Move an event to another category whenever it feels right. Once your new, larger stories are complete, take a break. Wait a day, if you'd like, and then read each aloud in the previous manner. Again, start with your A story, then read C, and finish with B.

Expanding your stories in stages like this can be a lot of work, but doing so may help you uncover meaningful events that you didn't realize were affecting you. Writing or typing answers makes the exercise specific and focuses your mind. Speaking each story aloud helps you to better understand how you're being affected emotionally. Going to the full length and depth of this exercise may bring up intense feelings, as might stopping part of the way through. Are you someone who normally completes a task, or do you stop yourself when something feels scary or like too much work? Again, there is no right way to do this exercise; it is intended only for your benefit and edification. How you do the exercise is entirely your choice.

My choice?! Of course, it's your choice. Almost everything you do is done by choice. Reading this book is a choice. Performing the exercise is a choice. The depth to which you perform it is a choice. No one will give you a demerit, if you stop at the first lists of three. You have the choice to analyze your feelings while reading your stories aloud or to shy away from the possible emotions. You have the choice to follow all or none of the instructions. In the same vein, you have the choice about which of your stories you will hold dearest to you.

The most important thing is to make each choice a *conscious* one.

Bring Your "A Game"

Life is change. Growth is optional. Choose wisely.
Karen Kaiser Clark

To exist is to change, to change is to mature, to mature is to go on creating oneself endlessly.
Henri Bergson

Every saint has a past, and every sinner has a future.
Oscar Wilde

Because things are the way they are, things will not stay the way they are.
Bertolt Brecht

No leader can be too far ahead of his followers.
Eleanor Roosevelt

Not being able to govern events, I govern myself.
Michel de Montaigne

CHAPTER 3

"I used to embrace stasis until I realized that made me a form of static cling."

Bring Your "A Game"

"A game" is a term primarily used when referring to performance in sports, but business has co-opted the saying. It implies you'll bring your best effort and all of your skill. You'll play hard and play to win. If you don't win, it won't be from lack of trying. You won't give up; you'll always be your best. You'll bring your "A game." Here, just like Mr. A and his A story, it refers to how you want to live your life. After all, which grade is better: A or C? Do you want to excel or simply be average? How do you want to live your life?

Hopefully, you've chosen to write your A, B and C stories and have considered them and lived with them for a while. Which do you prefer? Why? *Say your reasons out loud.* Some people may choose their worst story, because that's the one with which they are most comfortable and familiar. Giving your reasons voice will help you better understand them and, possibly, hear if they are patently absurd or detrimental. Preferring your C story would be unfortunate, but it's still your choice to make. People make bad decisions every day. However, I'd like to encourage you to make *conscious* choices, thoughtful choices, those not ruled by subconscious impulses or C story training. A conscious choice becomes more difficult to make badly. A conscious choice ensures you are taking some measure of responsibility in your life. You still may choose to cheat on your girlfriend, but you will have to own it as your decision. You can't blame your parents or your upbringing. *You made the decision!* You own the responsibility of your choice—and its outcome.

Most people, once they've completed the earlier exercise, will consider their day-to-day choices and the potential outcomes more deeply. Taking a few seconds to consider a decision's ramifications may help save your marriage, save your life, or save your soul. It will also help you take responsibility for your life, even if you allow your subconscious and C story training to choose your actions for you.

Continuing the exercise from the last chapter, take out each of your stories. They should be on separate pieces of paper, either handwritten or printed from your computer. If you wrote your stories in your book, tear or cut out your B and C stories. That's right; remove them from your book. The book is formatted in such a way that they can be torn out without losing important printed material. Do you have each story in front of you? Now, rip, tear or crumple up your C story. You may choose to burn it and make a ritual out of it. *Just be careful.* With a nod to modern times, feel free to put your C story in a shredder. The point is: *get rid of it. Choose* to get rid of it. If you have difficulty doing that, for any reason, you'll need to consider why. Why is it hard to let go? Is your subconscious stronger than your conscious self? Why hang on to the worst events of your life? They don't define you. *You can't let them define you!* If you can't let go of a written story, you're probably not trying hard enough to overcome the power those events hold on you. *Choose* to make them powerless. *Rip them up!* Rip up your C story!

Savor your choice to get rid of your C story. For most of you, it will be easy to do. For others, there may be some struggle. Others will not want to give up on a written story they've worked so hard on and whose events and power may give their life meaning, even if the meaning isn't one that supports a better life. Make the choice to dispose of that whole story. Be brave enough to throw it away. It's a simple, but powerful, act.

The events of your life will always be part of *your history*, but they *don't have to be part of your story now*. Once you've thrown away your C story, it should be easy to tear, rip, burn or shred your B story. *Who needs or wants a bland life?*

You will also want to rip out the pages with your B and C events listed. Rip, shred or burn them, but get rid of those pages, too.

Now, you're left with your A story. You should be proud of all the things you've accomplished, whether it was getting your GED, fixing a car engine, or raising a child as a single mom. Perhaps, you hold down a job and pay your rent on time. Be very proud of that. Do you take care of your elderly parents? Do you give to charity? Have you helped a little old lady across the street? Take heart in all of those things, those are actions that will help you moving forward. You can choose to live those things every day. We all have many, many acts and events of which we can be proud. Cherish each and every one. Cherish your A story.

Say aloud, "I choose A! I choose A! I choose A!" You've chosen to throw away the negative events in your life's history to focus on the best events, your proudest moments. Good for you. You may even want to add that new act to your A story.

Many authors suggest affirmations as a way to help their readers. Affirmations are fine, unless they become an empty regurgitation of words. If an affirmation brings you positive feeling, creating belief, it may be helpful. *But I believe your A story is far more powerful and helpful.* The difference between an affirmation and your A story is that *you know your A story is true*. You've spent a lot of time and effort on it, and you know it affects you positively. I suggest that you read your A story aloud *every day*. Reading it aloud each day will remind you of the good you've experienced and the positive value of your life. It will only take a few minutes. Focus on the good you've done and can do again.

I've told each of my A, B and C stories many times: certainly I've told them to myself. After fifty-one years, I finally understand that I can tell whichever story I choose, because each one is true. I can't lie to myself—the old "fake it, till you make it" ruse—because the subconscious knows when you're lying, and it will resist those lies. The subconscious also knows the truth, because it's been with you for the whole ride.

You must tell the truth. Fortunately, the subconscious doesn't mandate *which* truth you must tell. Once I stopped telling Mr. B's story and Mr. C's story and focused on my A story, I began enjoying life a lot more and looking forward to each new day. An affirmation may or may not feel like truth to you. Your A story is absolutely and unequivocally true.

If you're happy and living your best life, don't change a thing. Congratulations. If you're living something other than your best life; consider consciously talking louder. Find a safe place where you can shout, if you need to. "I choose A!" Your subconscious may be offended, but you should be offended at the havoc it has wreaked in your life thus far. You need to be offended! Be angry enough to talk back! If you don't, you'll continue to get what you've been getting and be at the mercy of your subconscious. And if that wasn't working for you before, it probably won't work any better going forward.

Get used to talking to yourself, aloud or internally, depending on your surroundings and circumstance, when negative, non-supportive thoughts come into your mind. If you don't, your subconscious will continue to dominate. The subconscious is powerful, so you have to be more powerful *consciously*. Don't allow unhelpful thoughts to linger. Like a rotten apple, it only takes one to ruin the rest. Get rid of a rotten thought and keep it out consciously. Don't allow yourself to abdicate life choices to your subconscious. Talk loud. Stomp around. Do whatever it takes to get the attention of your subconscious. Show it that you're the boss. Because if you aren't consciously the boss, your subconscious will be your boss, and your life will continue to be stuck by whatever is in there sticking it to you. You must demand that your conscious self dictates what your mind hears and believes.

When someone asks you about yourself, please tell your best story. Always make the choice to say the best things you can about yourself. Don't worry about sounding arrogant; most of us have the far worse problem of downplaying our successes and our significance. If you are already supremely confident, you're probably not reading this book anyway. Understand that every time you shy away from or deny your A story, you reinforce what is left—your B and C stories. Give them your A story! Bring your "A game"! Choose consciously!

My wife is a big part of my A story. She's one of the most supportive, positive people in the world—especially with me. I've been fortunate to meet someone so communicative about her love for me and my good traits. She tells my A story every day and does it far better than I do. Sadly, at first, I found it difficult to believe her when she said such nice things about me. It actually annoyed me sometimes, because I thought she was lying. *Talk about C story training!* I thought she was just *playing* nice, rather than *being* nice. I wasn't used to such positivity and didn't know how to handle it. I was loved more than I knew how to love myself, and her love has helped me choose a better story and way to live. May you all be so lucky to find such a great partner, but whether you do or not, be your own best partner by focusing on your A story.

Surround yourself whenever possible with positive people, people that respect and care about you. The more you respect and care for yourself, which is a big part of bringing your "A game," the easier it will be to find others that will do so, too.

When you're around people that expect good things from you, you tend to live up to their expectations and increase your own expectations, rather than searching for excuses not to do so. Being human, I have my share of bad habits. One in particular surprises me for its disgustingness. *I sometimes spit in public!* Ugh. Growing up in rural Maine with a family that played sports and worked outdoors, I saw a whole lot of spitting, and it became a habit of mine. Strangely, despite attending good schools and working in a suit and tie, I continued spitting and never thought about how appalling that behavior is. Now that I've *considered it consciously*, I understand how incredibly

---

rude it is to anyone within sight or that will soon be walking in my path.

Improving my life and the lives of those around me is part of my "A game," as is writing this book. In the exploration of the ideas contained herein, I've discovered a technique that helps me reduce bad habits, like spitting, and emotional blockages. I use it as a reminder for my wife when she gets nervous about money issues. I use it for my mom when she's burdened by worry. It's a simple technique that anyone can use to help live a better, more centered life.

The technique can help you bring your "A game."

What Don't I Have to Do?

Life is the sum of all your choices.
Albert Camus

The strongest principle of growth lies in human choice.
George Eliot

Destiny is not a matter of chance, it is a matter of choice; it is not a thing to be waited for, it is a thing to be achieved.
William Jennings Bryan

The last, if not the greatest, of the human freedoms: to choose their own attitude in any given circumstance.
Bruno Bettelheim

The wonderful thing about saints is that they were human. They lost their tempers … were egotistical or impatient in their turns, made mistakes and regretted them. Still they went on doggedly blundering toward heaven.
Phyllis McGinley

I am seeking, I am striving, I am in it with all my heart.
Vincent van Gogh

CHAPTER 4

"Now that I understand I'm not that important, I feel like I can have some real impact in the world."

What Don't I Have to Do?

Please say aloud: *What don't I have to do?* Isn't that a beautifully simple sentence? It asks an innocuous, nonthreatening question that is easy to answer and can be answered in innumerable ways. You don't have to be scared of the question, because it gives you permission *not to do something*. What could be better than that? It doesn't require anything of you. There's no pressure to perform. It doesn't imply you must do something in order to get a certain result, but it can be very powerful in helping you strip away behaviors and emotions that may be holding you back in life.

Notice the question isn't: *What shouldn't I do?* That question implies you're already doing something wrong, that there's something you could feel guilty about doing. *You shouldn't be doing that!* Who hasn't heard that growing up?

Ask yourself instead: *What don't I have to do?* That gives you permission to give up whatever you choose. *Permission.* You simply ask the question and answers will come spontaneously. If you decide to stop doing a particular act, or give up a negative emotion, it will be because of your *conscious decision-making.* There is no negative motivation due to guilt. Just give something up that you already know you don't need. It is far easier psychologically to give up something than it is to force yourself to change behavior you may have done for years and years.

To explain further, let's only briefly go back to my spitting habit. When I'm tempted to let one fly, I ask myself, "What don't I have to do?" My answer could be anything, but, at that moment, it is likely to be, "I don't have to spit in public." And, despite the habit built over decades, it becomes easy not to spit. I simply give myself permission, so it becomes easier to *choose* not to spit. I become conscious of the disgusting act and its potential outcomes, none of which are good, and I give myself permission to not do it.

Okay, so much for that bad habit. Let's consider three less graphic areas where this simple sentence might be helpful.

Blaming – I doubt that blaming someone or something has ever helped anyone in the long run, although you wouldn't know it by listening to our politicians. Blaming others may momentarily relieve you of responsibility, but the responsibility to have a good, happy life is always yours and always will be. No one can achieve happiness, contentment or success for you.

My dad was a master of blaming others for unwanted outcomes, like my tractor incident. The incident wasn't his fault, but I was young and didn't understand his instructions. *Things happen.* He never blamed me with words, but left me to blame myself, which may be just as bad. Despite many talents and great qualities, he had difficulties owning up to his own responsibilities in a number of areas, like his drinking and failed marriage.

He could be very judgmental, hurtful, and tough to be around, but I presume he did the best he was able. He was born during the depression and grew up poor. His older brother had died before he was born. He had C story training that he never seemed to get past. He suffered from low self-esteem, although I doubt he was aware of it or could ever admit it, and he likely drank to escape his inner turmoil. Blaming others helped him skirt responsibility, rather than face his own culpability.

Had my father been able to face his demons in a constructive way, I think he could have been a great man. He was often generous and charming. He was funny, smart, creative and talented. He ran businesses of many types and was usually successful. He helped grow our home town as a Selectman and became a State Representative.

People may create obstacles or unwanted results for you, by choice, accident, or omission. You can immediately blame someone, or you can *choose* to focus on how you go over, through or around any obstacle to get the results you desire. You can use your energy and intelligence to improve yourself and take positive action. If you're a blamer, ask yourself: *What don't I have to do?*

Maybe your answer will be: *I don't have to lash out with blame.* A simple question and answer may give you time to consider the ramifications of your actions. You can give yourself permission to not do something that can only be harmful to others, to your relationship with them, and to yourself.

Fear – Fear is valuable when you're being chased by a man-eater or when you have an upcoming chemistry exam for which you haven't studied. It can be greatly motivational. Unfortunately, fear is often misplaced and debilitating. Fearing the unknown and unknowable is worse than useless; doing so draws huge amounts of energy away from finding a solution that might actually alleviate whatever is causing you angst in the first place.

I've succumbed to irrational fears many times. Even when I was too young to seriously consider marriage, I was afraid I would follow in my father's marital footsteps and be destined for a painful divorce. That was my C story training and one reason it took me until I was fifty to fully accept a woman's love and to be able to love her back. Obviously, such a deep-seated fear will require more than one question and answer to conquer it. However, had I known the simple, magic question, I might not have waited four years to ask my wife to marry me. *What don't I have to do? I don't have to be afraid of the unknowable. I don't have to follow in my father's every footstep. Better yet, I don't have to be afraid of love.*

Speaking of my wife, she can at times become fearful about money matters. *Who can't?* Although she's successful, smart and hardworking, she runs her own business and her cash flows vary. In her nervous moments, I've started asking her, "What don't you have to do?" in a loving and, sometimes, downright silly way. She smiles, sheepish, and answers, "Worry." Then we both laugh. She feels better, because she knows she really doesn't have to worry and that we're doing fine, and she's reminded that her fear isn't helpful or based on reality. It's become a game for us and a pressure release whenever stress rises. Asking the question makes me feel like I've been a good partner, because I ask her out of love, just the way you must ask yourself. I give her permission not to be afraid, and she gives herself the same permission.

Worry – This seems to be my mother's favorite thing to do. She and I have discussed this one a lot over the years. Worry is based on fear, but worry *implies* that the worrier has some ability to change something or someone. It implies they have power or control far above any actuality, which may be why worriers like to worry. In some perverse way, worrying helps them feel like they have control and power when they typically have none. If you have control, you generally don't worry. If you have power, you don't need to worry. *Why would you?* It is only those who have neither that worry. On the other hand, if you have no power to change someone or a situation, why bother worrying? *There's nothing you can do! You're powerless!* Simply admit it, have a laugh, and move on to something useful.

> **God grant me the serenity to accept the things I cannot change, the power to change the things I can, and the wisdom to know the difference.**
> Frederic Neibuhr

Worrying is worse than a waste of time and energy; it actually detracts from the world's potential. Worriers short-change themselves, their loved ones, and the world. They could offer so much more by being in the moment, communicating, and working to create solutions rather than spinning metaphorical wheels, wasting energy.

That said, we've all had bouts of worrying. When my mom starts going on about something she's agonizing over without any way to affect it, I ask her the question. "What don't you have to do?" She didn't understand right away, so I explained the reason for the question. Because she's a great sport, once I had explained the futility of her worrying, she laughed at herself and felt better. She recognized her tendency and from where it came. (There's that C story training again!) The awareness she gained from my asking that simple question helped her become conscious of a behavior that doesn't serve her or help anyone else.

Thankfully, everyone in my family has a good sense of humor. I just hope they still will after they read this book!

We all have issues with which we deal: bad habits, harmful tendencies, and negative emotions. Asking a simple question won't cure them instantly, but asking the question can lead to answers and understanding and may give you permission to start changing for the better.

People will answer the question in different ways under different circumstances. The question is only for you. What matters is how *you* answer it. By considering the question and your individual answer, you may surprise yourself and learn something valuable.

What the question doesn't do is give you permission to avoid responsibility! You can't use the technique to get out of mowing the lawn, brushing your teeth, or going to work. Face it; there are things we just can't avoid— bathing being one of the foremost.

Examples of how the question *might* be answered follow:

What don't I have to do? **I don't have to yell at my kids when I get angry.**

What don't I have to do? **I don't have to feel afraid to meet new people.**

What don't I have to do? **I don't have to take out my anger on others or myself.**

What don't I have to do? **I don't have to drink that fourth beer that always gets me into trouble.**

What don't I have to do? **I don't have to be a victim of my subconscious.**

What don't I have to do? **I don't have to take all the credit for success at work.**

What don't I have to do? **I don't have to worry about things I can't control.** (Are you listening, Mom?)

What don't I have to do? **I don't have to feel like a victim.**

What don't I have to do? **I don't have to objectify women by surfing porn.**

What don't I have to do? **I don't have to smoke a cigarette after lunch.**

What don't I have to do? **I don't have to be afraid of love.** (This is my personal favorite.)

What don't I have to do? **I don't have to feel ashamed of attaining great wealth.**

What don't I have to do? **I don't have to feel ashamed about showing and sharing my abilities.**

What don't I have to do? **I don't have to be quiet when I really need to speak up.**

What don't I have to do? **I don't have to focus on the negative experiences in my past.**

What don't I have to do? **I don't have to compare myself to anyone else.**

What don't I have to do? **I don't have to live a C life.**

However you answer the question, please voice your responses in full sentences whenever possible. Voicing helps you to be clear and to counter any self doubts.

Live Your Best Life

If the only prayer you say in your whole life is "Thank you,"
that would suffice.
Meister Eckhart

Joy is the simplest form of gratitude.
Karl Barth

My friends are my estate.
Emily Dickinson

What a wonderful life I've had! I only wish I'd realized it
sooner.
Colette

Reflect upon your present blessings, of which every man
has many; not on your past misfortunes, of which all men
have some.
Charles Dickens

He who laughs, lasts!
Mary Pettibone Poole

CHAPTER 5

"The happier I become, the luckier I get."

Live Your Best Life

I am the luckiest guy in the world, and I have felt that way for more years than I can remember. Despite a few bumps in the road of life we all travel, I feel blessed every day because of my father, mother, brothers, sister, grandparents, nieces, nephews, aunts, uncles, friends, teachers, coaches, wife and everyone else who has helped make me who I am.

My father passed away last year, and I miss him every day, despite what I felt were psychological injuries from my youth. He did the best he could, and I long ago forgave him for not meeting my high expectations, just as I've forgiven myself for not meeting them, too. Unfortunately, forgiveness was something he could not do for himself.

My mother is one of the sweetest and kindest people I know. She has a great sense of humor and is generous and loving. That she couldn't always protect me and sometimes succumbs to her fears is understandable—no one has ever reached perfection—but she bravely learns and grows as a person every day. At a vibrant eighty-one years of age she is more amazing than she knows.

My parents have played the most important roles in me becoming who I am. As I've become more comfortable with myself, I've appreciated them more and more. They can be proud of what they've done to raise a loving, healthy family, and offer the best they possessed to the world. I hope all of you have been as fortunate as I and will appreciate the people who have helped you along your way.

None of us deserves an excuse for doing bad things to anyone, but no one can shirk responsibility for their own growth and life choices. *What don't I have to do? I, Dean Erickson, don't have to blame or depend on anyone for my success, failure, happiness or anything else.* As an adult, I take responsibility for my own care and my own actions. I encourage you to do the same.

I've also made a lot of mistakes. There is no way not to; mistakes come with the territory. The beautiful thing is that every day until you die you get another chance to live your life the best way you can. You can choose to remind yourself of the best aspects of your life or the worst. For your sake and everyone else's, always choose the best in order to support your personal growth. The healthier you become, the healthier the world becomes. Help people rise to your level instead of stooping to theirs.

Given the preponderance of accessible information, there are innumerable resources for self-improvement. Use what is available in terms of self-development opportunities, whether helpful ideas derive from a book, the Internet, a psychiatrist, or a seminar. Simply remember: *studying to become better is no excuse not to be better now!*

The exercises and suggestions in this book have helped me and others. The techniques are not deeply researched, but they are deeply reasoned. They can help you quickly and continue to help you throughout your life.

I trust by now you have developed your A story and have consciously decided to "throw away" your lesser stories. Instead of using impersonal affirmations, remind yourself of very personal successes daily to help you know that you can create more. You've succeeded before, it is logical you can succeed again. You've been happy before, it is logical you can be happy now and in the future. Tell yourself the truth, it is always the best policy, but please tell yourself the best truth you can. Negativity can only breed negativity, so avoid your B and C stories and the people who spout theirs. Affirm the best aspects of your life in order to create more.

I don't believe in "fake it, till you make it." Why fake it? You always know when you're faking it! Simply believe in yourself based on the previous successes in your A story, and take action to succeed again.

"Every day in every way, I am getting better and better" is another well-worn affirmation. If the statement helps you, by all means, use it. However, it doesn't ring totally true to me. I *know* my back isn't getting any younger or better, nor are my knees. Can you honestly say you are getting better in *every* way? Why try to convince yourself of an untruth? You'll use your time more wisely by reciting your A story and taking your personal successes to heart.

It is easy to hear or read the news and become disillusioned, but the unusual is news; the bad or ugly is unusual; the bad or ugly is news. Big and little kindnesses and heroic acts occur every second of every day all around the world, but we don't often hear about them. Good gets taken for granted because it's commonplace. Sometimes that happens in one's life, too. Please don't focus on the bad or negative in your history, just so you can engender sympathy, get attention, or feel important. *You already are important!* You're flesh and blood, and you have an opportunity to experience happiness, make friends, and create good in the world every day. Everything you do can be valuable to someone. *How much more important do you need to be?* Focus on the best things you've experienced, so you can better appreciate your life and create more good in it. Just because the news focuses negatively, that doesn't mean you should.

I believe in *gratitude informed by realism*. Pollyannas are unrealistic and too easily disappointed. Not everything will happen for you just because you want it and dream about it, but good outcomes are certainly more likely if you *believe in yourself and take positive action*. The exercises and suggestions in this book can help you know and appreciate your enormous personal value and free you to create more success and happiness.

We all have stories we tell about ourselves to others and to ourselves. I hope this book will help you illuminate your best story and understand why it's critical to focus on that story. If you will, you'll be more likely to improve your life and encourage others to do the same for themselves.

And, if you learn to make your choices consciously, I bet you'll choose your A story, "A game," and A life every time.

Appendices

Appendix A

When I did the exercise in Chapter 2, I came up with the answers listed below. Mine aren't for comparison; the exercise is about you and *your* story. Notice that each of my answers is short and to the point, saying just enough *for me to know what it means*.

Write down the three *best* things or events that have happened in your life.

1. high school championship
2. marriage
3. friendships

Write down the three *worst* things or events that have happened in your life.

1. parents' divorce
2. back/health issues
3. father's alcoholism

Write down any three *other* things or events that have happened in your life.

1. Brown graduation
2. Wall Street
3. novel

Appendix B

Write down the *best* things or events that have happened in your life.

1.

2.

3.

4.

5.

6.

7.

8.

9.

10.

11.

12.

13.

14.

15.

Appendix B (cont'd)

Write down the *worst* things or events that have happened in your life.

1.

2.

3.

4.

5.

6.

7.

8.

9.

10.

11.

12.

13.

14.

15.

Appendix B (cont'd)

Write down *other* things or events that have happened in your life.

1.

2.

3.

4.

5.

6.

7.

8.

9.

10.

11.

12.

13.

14.

15.

Appendix C

MY A STORY

_____

_____

_____

_____

_____

_____

_____

_____

_____

_____

_____

_____

_____

_____

_____

_____

_____

Appendix C (cont'd)

MY A STORY

_____

_____

_____

_____

_____

_____

_____

_____

_____

_____

_____

_____

_____

_____

_____

_____

Appendix C (cont'd)

MY A STORY

_____

_____

_____

_____

_____

_____

_____

_____

_____

_____

_____

_____

_____

_____

_____

_____

_____

Appendix C (cont'd)

MY A STORY

_____

_____

_____

_____

_____

_____

_____

_____

_____

_____

_____

_____

_____

_____

_____

Appendix C (cont'd)

MY A STORY

_____

_____

_____

_____

_____

_____

_____

_____

_____

_____

_____

_____

_____

_____

_____

Appendix C (cont'd)

MY A STORY

_____

_____

_____

_____

_____

_____

_____

_____

_____

_____

_____

_____

_____

Appendix C (cont'd)

MY B STORY

_____

_____

_____

_____

_____

_____

_____

_____

_____

_____

_____

_____

_____

_____

_____

_____

Appendix C (cont'd)

MY B STORY

_____

_____

_____

_____

_____

_____

_____

_____

_____

_____

_____

_____

_____

_____

_____

_____

Appendix C (cont'd)

MY B STORY

_____

_____

_____

_____

_____

_____

_____

_____

_____

_____

_____

_____

_____

_____

_____

_____

Appendix C (cont'd)

MY B STORY

_____

_____

_____

_____

_____

_____

_____

_____

_____

_____

_____

_____

_____

_____

Appendix C (cont'd)

MY B STORY

_____

_____

_____

_____

_____

_____

_____

_____

_____

_____

_____

_____

_____

_____

_____

Appendix C (cont'd)

MY B STORY

_____

_____

_____

_____

_____

_____

_____

_____

_____

_____

_____

_____

_____

_____

_____

Appendix C (cont'd)

MY C STORY

_____

_____

_____

_____

_____

_____

_____

_____

_____

_____

_____

_____

_____

Appendix C (cont'd)

MY C STORY

Appendix C (cont'd)

MY C STORY

_____

_____

_____

_____

_____

_____

_____

_____

_____

_____

_____

_____

_____

_____

_____

Appendix C (cont'd)

MY C STORY

_____

_____

_____

_____

_____

_____

_____

_____

_____

_____

_____

_____

_____

_____

_____

Appendix C (cont'd)

MY C STORY

_____

_____

_____

_____

_____

_____

_____

_____

_____

_____

_____

_____

_____

_____

_____

Appendix C (cont'd)

MY C STORY

_____

_____

_____

_____

_____

_____

_____

_____

_____

_____

_____

_____

_____

_____

_____

About the Author

About the Author

Dean Erickson is the founder and CEO of Bionic Capital LLC, a registered investment advisory firm which specializes in wealth management and philanthropic investment solutions. He started on Wall Street as an options trader and risk arbitrageur before leaving to become an actor. After guest starring on *Frasier,* starring as Gabriel Knight in the awarding-winning video game *The Beast Within*, and starring in several lesser Shakespearean productions, he turned his focus to writing. While multiple movie manuscripts accumulated dust, he worked on a mystery novel for ten years, ultimately completing *No One Laughs at a Dead Clown* under the name, DC Erickson. After a computer glitch caused the loss of his outline for novel number two, he turned to the self-help genre, maybe to help himself recover. This book is the result and was published a few short months later. Prophetically, he was voted Most Versatile by his high school senior class a long, long time ago. More recently, he was elected to the Midcoast Maine Sports Hall of Fame.

He lives in California with his wonderful wife, Lisa.

Made in the USA
Charleston, SC
14 December 2010